Contents

Brazil

Key
- ☐ Land above 1000m
- ☐ Land above 0m/sea level
- ▨ Rainforest
- ● Capital
- ● Important cities

North

Equator

Amazon River

Brazilia

Iguaçu Falls   São Paulo

ATLANTIC
OCEAN

Brazil is in South America. It is the fifth largest country in the world. The name Brazil comes from a tree which grows there and gives us Brazil nuts.

A Visit to
BRAZIL

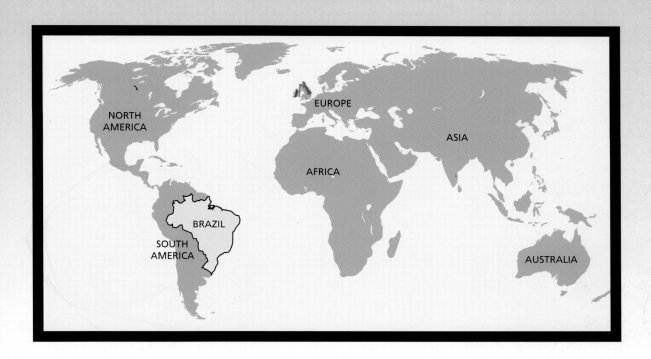

NORTH
AMERICA

EUROPE

ASIA

AFRICA

BRAZIL

SOUTH
AMERICA

AUSTRALIA

Peter & Connie Roop

SOME INFORMATION IN
THIS RESOURCE IS
OUT OF DATE

Heinemann

First published in Great Britain by Heinemann Library
Halley Court, Jordan Hill, Oxford OX2 8EJ
a division of Reed Educational and Professional Publishing Ltd.
Heinemann is a registered trademark of Reed Educational & Professional Publishing Limited.

OXFORD FLORENCE PRAGUE MADRID ATHENS
MELBOURNE AUCKLAND KUALA LUMPUR SINGAPORE TOKYO
IBADAN NAIROBI KAMPALA JOHANNESBURG GABORONE
PORTSMOUTH NH CHICAGO MEXICO CITY SAO PAULO

Designed by AMR
Illustrations by Art Construction
Colour Reproduction by Dot Gradations, U.K.
Printed in Hong Kong by Wing King Tong Co., Ltd.

02 01 00 99
10 9 8 7 6 5 4 3 2 1

ISBN 0 431 08321 5
This title is also available in a hardback library edition (ISBN 0 431 08312 6).

Acknowledgements
The Publishers would like to thank the following for permission to reproduce photographs:
LUPE CUNHA: pp 20, 26; Hutchison Library: p23, Errington p12, J Horner p9, C Macarthy p22,
J von Puttkamer p5; Tony Morrison: pp10, 11, 13, 16, 17, 25, 27, South American Pictures pp6,
14, 19, 28, 29; Trip: S Grant pp7, 24, T Lester p18, C Phillips p15, J Wender p21; ZEFA: J Ramid p8

Cover photograph reproduced with permission of Sue Cunningham Photographic.

Our thanks to Rob Alcraft for his comments in the preparation of this book.

Every effort has been made to contact holders of any material reproduced in this book.
Any omissions will be rectified in subsequent printings if notice is given to the Publisher.

Any words appearing in bold, **like this**, are explained in the Glossary.

The first people in Brazil were the
native Indians. Then people from all over
the world went to live in Brazil. They
came from Europe, Africa and Asia.

5

Land

Brazil has **rainforests**, rivers, **grasslands** and beaches. Most of Brazil is south of the **equator**. Brazil has **tropical** weather.

Brazil has more people and land than any other country in South America. Most Brazilians live in or around the cities.

The Amazon River flows through Brazil. It is the second largest river in the world. One thousand rivers run into the Amazon River.

Iguaçu Falls is in Brazil. It is one of the most beautiful **waterfalls** in the world. It is on the **border** between Brazil and Argentina.

Homes

Brasilia is the **capital** city, but São Paulo is Brazil's largest city. It is one of the largest cities in the world.

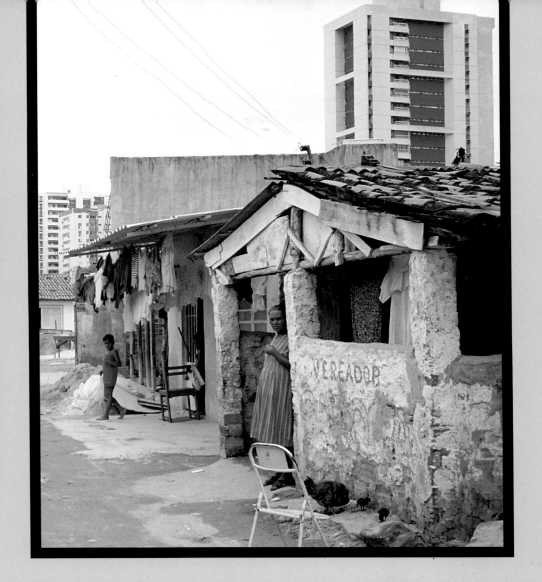

Brazil has rich people but it has many more poor people. They live in **favelas** outside the big cities. There are some Brazilians who live in the **rainforest**.

Food

People have moved to Brazil from all around the world. They took with them many different **recipes**. Most of these use rice, beef, pork, fruit, vegetables or beans.

Feijoada came from Africa and is the most popular food in Brazil. It is a stew of pork, beef, sausage, bacon and black beans. It is served with sliced oranges.

Clothes

Brazil has a **tropical climate**. It is usually warm so people wear light, cool clothing. **Native Indians** wear **traditional** clothes in the wet **rainforest**.

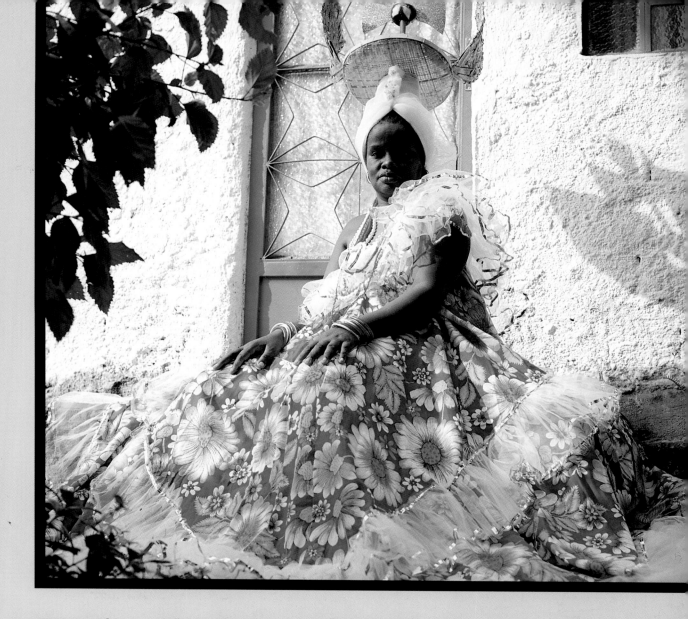

Brazilians have many **festivals** and holidays. This is when they like to dress up in colourful costumes.

Work

Farmers in Brazil grow more sugar cane and coffee than any other country in the world. There are also lots of farmers or ranchers who have beef cattle.

Workers dig **iron ore** out of the ground to make steel. People in **factories** make steel, cloth, cars and other **products**. Brazil sells many of these products to other countries.

Transport

Brazilians travel by car, bus and truck.
In the crowded cities people share cars
to save money and time.

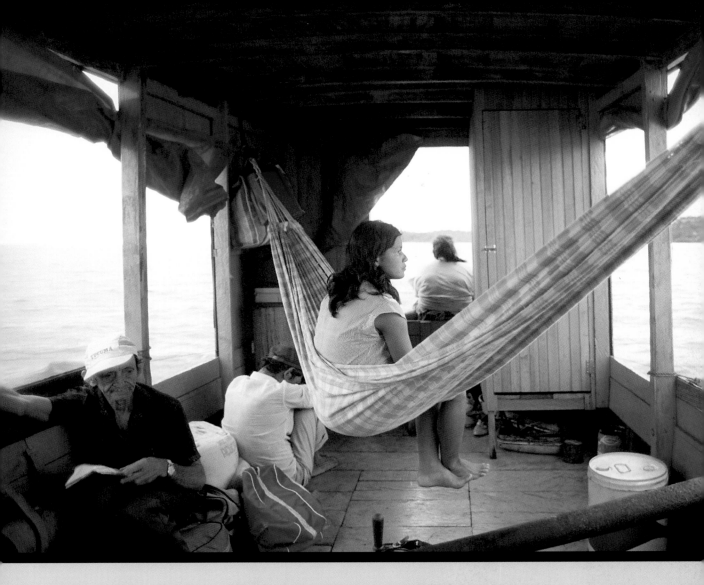

The Amazon River is like a giant road into the centre of Brazil. People travel in the Amazon **Rainforest** by boat or helicopter.

Language

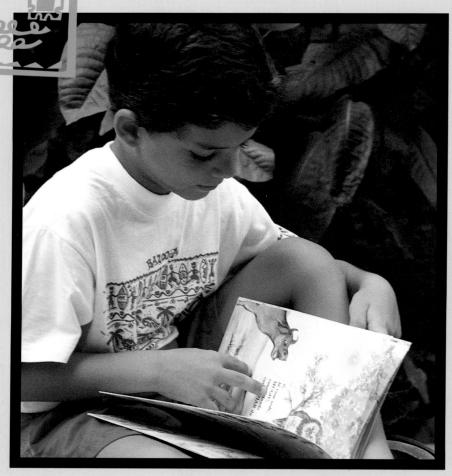

Portuguese is Brazil's national language. Explorers from Portugal took it to Brazil 500 years ago. People also speak native Indian and African languages.

The first Brazilians were the **native Indians**. People from Europe moved to Brazil 500 years ago. They took with them African **slaves**. Today many people from Asia are moving to Brazil.

School

Most children go to school from the age of 6 to 16. They study Portuguese, history, maths, science and art. Primary school ends before noon each day.

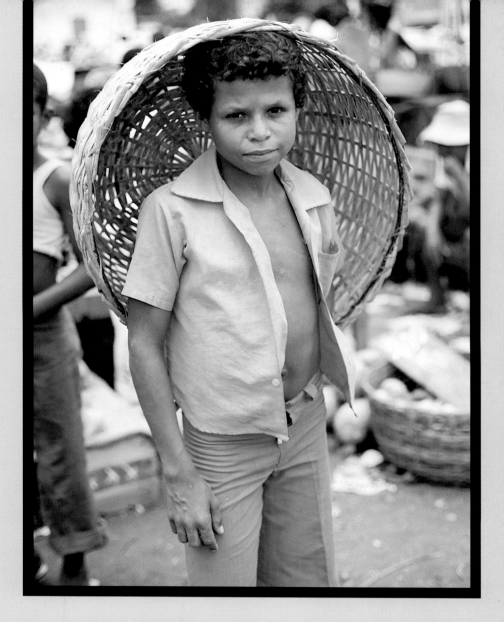

Some Brazilian children are too poor to go to school. They must work to help feed their families.

Free time

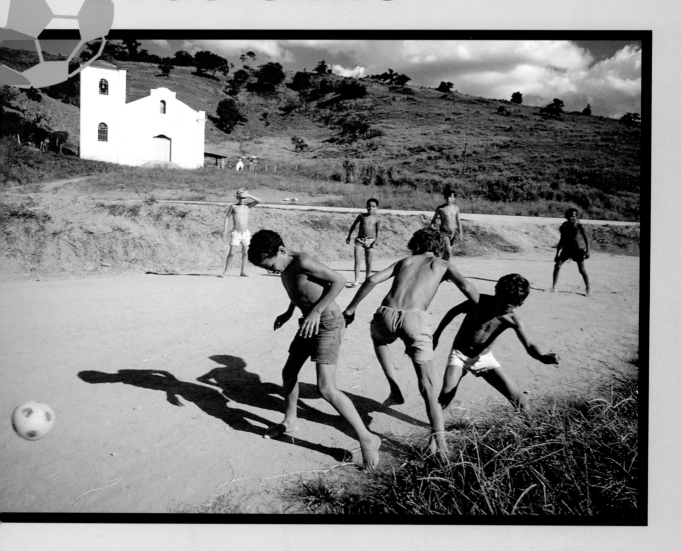

Football (soccer) is called futebol. It is the most popular sport in Brazil. All Brazilian children, rich and poor, play futebol.

Capoeira is a Brazilian sport. It is like a fight, a dance and judo all in one. Other popular sports are basketball, volleyball, tennis and jogging.

Celebrations

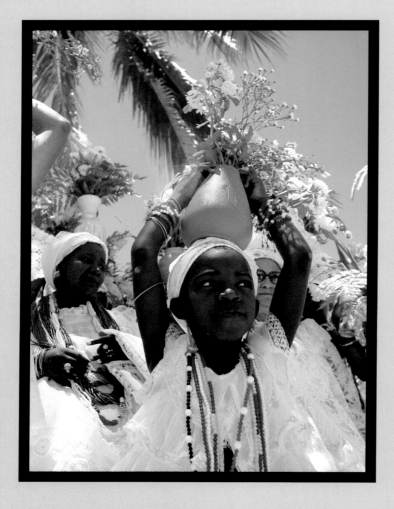

Lemnaja is a Brazilian New Year's celebration. On New Year's Eve, people go to the beach. They give presents to Lemnaja, the goddess of the sea.

Carnival is Brazil's biggest **festival**. It takes place about six weeks before Easter. There are **parades** through the noisy streets.

The Arts

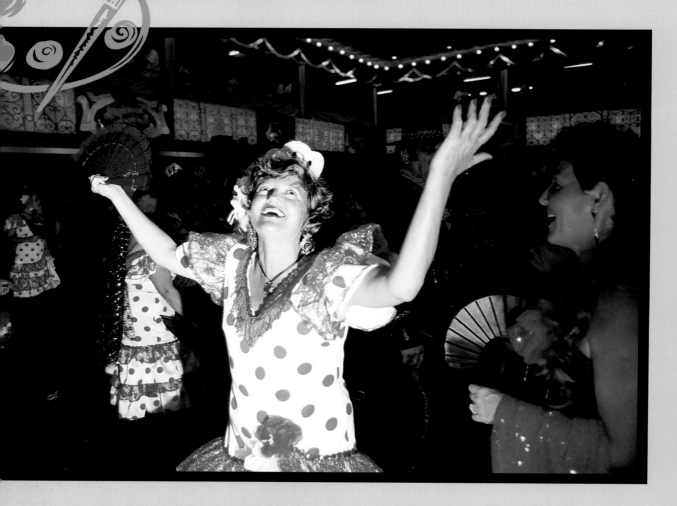

Brazilians play music learned from the **native Indians**, Africa and from Europe. People also like to play and sing choros or folk tunes.

The berimbaus is a Brazilian **instrument**.
It has one string and is played with a bow.
Other popular instruments are guitars,
banjos, drums and maracas.

Factfile

Name	The full name of Brazil is the Federal Republic of Brazil.
Capital	The **capital** city is Brasilia.
Language	Most Brazilians speak Portuguese.
Population	There are 160 million people living in Brazil.
Money	Instead of the dollar or pound, Brazilians have the real.
Religions	Most Brazilians are Catholic or Protestant.
Products	Brazil produces more coffee and sugar cane than any other country.

Words you can learn

oi	hello
tchau	goodbye
obrigato	thank you
sim	yes
nao	no
um	one
dois	two
tres	three

Glossary

border	where two countries meet
capital	the city where the government is based
climate	the normal type of weather for the area
equator	an imaginary line around the earth dividing it into a northern half and a southern half
factories	places where things are made
favelas	large areas covered in small, roughly made huts where people live
festival	a big celebration planned for lots of people to enjoy together
grasslands	large flat areas where grasses are the only plants which grow
instrument	something which makes music
iron ore	the rock which contains iron
native Indians	the first people who were living in Brazil
parade	a group of people on show, dancing or walking together
products	things which are grown, taken from the earth, made by hand or made in a factory
rainforest	a thick forest that stays green all year and which has rain almost every day
recipe	a set of directions for making food
slave	a person who is taken from their home and family and sold to another person to do work
traditional	the way something has been done or made for a long time
tropical	hot and humid
waterfall	where water falls down the side of a mountain

Index